A Sensible Approach to Fasting and Prayer

A Sensible Approach to Fasting and Prayer

by Dr. Rachel V. Jeffries

**Christian Literature & Artwork
A BOLD TRUTH Publication**

Shut Your Mouth
Copyright © 2020 by Dr. Rachel V. Jeffries
Rachel Jeffries International Ministries
ISBN 13: 978-1-949993-58-5

FIRST EDITION

BOLD TRUTH PUBLISHING
(Christian Literature & Artwork)
606 West 41st, Ste. 4
Sand Springs, Oklahoma 74063
www.BoldTruthPublishing.com
boldtruthbooks@yahoo.com

Available from Amazon.com and other retail outlets. Orders by U.S. trade bookstores and wholesalers.

Quantity sales special discounts are available on quantity purchases by corporations, associations, and others. For details, contact the publisher at the address above.

Cover Art & Design by Aaron Jones

All rights reserved under International Copyright Law. All contents and/or cover art and design may not be reproduced in whole or in part in any form without the express written consent of the Author.

Printed in the USA.
09 20   10 9 8 7 6 5 4 3 2 1

Unless otherwise indicated, all Scripture quotations are taken from the KING JAMES VERSION (KJV): KING JAMES VERSION, public domain.

Copyright © 1995 by The Zondervan Corporation and the Lockman Foundation. Scripture marked AMP are taken from THE AMPLIFIED BIBLE, Old Testament Copyright © 1965, 1987, by the Zondervan Corporation. The amplified New Testament copyright, © 1958, 1987 by The Lockman Foundation. Used by permission.

"Scripture quotations marked NIV are taken from the Holy Bible, New International Version®. NIV®. Copyright © 1973, 1978, 1984 by International Bible Society. Used by permission of Zondervan. All rights reserved."

Table of Contents

introduction
by Dr. Rachel V. Jeffries..*i*

Chapter 1
What is Fasting? 1

Chapter 2
History of Fasting 9

Chapter 3
Is Fasting for Today? 17

Chapter 4
Purpose of Fasting 19

Chapter 5
Wrong Purposes-Not Honored 25

Chapter 6
What Does God Accept? 33

Chapter 7
How Long Should I Fast? 37

Chapter 8
What Did Jesus Say? 41

Chapter 9
Corporate Oneness 45

Chapter 10
Rewards of Fasting 49

Chapter 11
Health and Fasting 55

Contents

Chapter 12
Common Sense in Fasting 59

Chapter 13
How to Break a Fast 67

Chapter 14
A Fasted Life 71

Conclusion 75

About the Author 77

Contact Information 78

Introduction

Maybe you are wondering if this is a book about keeping your mouth pure with your words. Even though this information is in the book, I feel the subject is much more thorough. I believe there has been much misunderstanding about **fasting and prayer.** Some Scriptures place prayer first and then fasting while other Scriptures say fasting first. Lest we get technical about it, I really feel they go together like hand and glove.

Fasting done the wrong way can be totally ineffective, fleshly and therefore, profit nothing. We are in perilous times and we need to know how to correctly and effectively pray and fast for our nation. The history of fasting in the Bible and its effects are named. Some fasting was nonproductive, while others heard from God so clearly as they obeyed God in very effective Spirit-led fasting and prayer. The meaning of the word *fasting* is clarified in this writing.

Let us sharpen our tools in these times. May the **Holy Spirit reveal** to you just what you need to know to be made free of any bondage of past teachings, and misunderstandings. I pray for each of you to digest this knowledge and follow God's Spirit and obey what He is saying for you to do.

Chapter 1
What is Fasting?

Strong's Concordance says *'fasting'* is to **cover the mouth.** Not only are we to watch what goes into our mouths, but also to be careful what comes out of our mouths. Strong's also says to abstain, **abstinence from food and without food.** If we fast food and keep putting things into our minds which is not edifying or pertaining to life and godliness our fasting is in vain. There may be some things that mean too much to you, then you need to offer that up to God in order to get control of your flesh. Fasting is for us to bring our flesh under God's power through prayer while we abstain from eating.

A lot of us have not known much about fasting and prayer. It has seemed to be a mystery to some. We want to do what is right, but may not understand the purpose of prayer and fasting. Maybe you have felt it was to move the hand of God concerning a need you have. While God is working, it is because you are more sensitive to hear and see what He is doing. To fast places us in subjection to the Holy Spirit and makes us more sensitive to hear His Voice. Fasting without Faith is no good. If we are fasting and speaking harmful things, we are hindering our fast.

Isaiah 58:6 AMP teaches much about fasting. *[Rather] is not this the fast that I have chosen: to loose the bonds of wickedness, to undo the bands of wickedness, to undo the bands of the yoke, to let the oppressed go free, and that you break every [enslaving] yoke?*

I loved what the Message Bible has to say in *Isaiah 58*. God is speaking about the Jews and is saying to all appearances they're a nation of right-living people, law abiding, God honoring. *They ask me, 'What's the right thing to do?' and love having me on their side. But they also complain, 'Why do we fast and you don't look our way?' Why do we humble ourselves and you don't even notice?'* "Well, here's why: *The bottom line is your fast days profit. You drive your employees much too hard. You fast, but you swing a mean fist. The kind of fasting you do won't get your prayers off the ground. Do you think this is the kind of fast day I'm after a day to show humility? To put on a pious long face and parade around solemnly in black? Do you call that fasting, a fast day that I, God, would like? This is the kind of fast day I'm after: to break the chains of injustice, get rid of exploitation in the workplace, free the oppressed, cancel debts. What I am interested in seeing you do is: Shar-*

What is Fasting?

ing your food with the hungry, inviting the homeless poor man into your homes, Putting clothes on the shivering ill-clad, being available to your own families. Do this and the light will turn on, and your lives will turn around at once. Your righteousness will pave your way. The God of Glory will secure your passage, then when you pray, God will answer. You'll call out for help and I'll say, 'Here I am.'

A few years ago my co-worker and I were on a trip in California. We felt led to fast TV and the radio for a week or more. Since we were on a fast of the TV and radio, we did not get the news that the highway we were to travel on was closed due to a bizarre happening. We noticed no cars were on the freeway and in California something has to be wrong if there are no cars on the freeway. We kept going, not realizing we were going to be stopped with traffic backed up for miles. We noticed as we drove all exits were closed not allowing us to get off and find out what was going on. There was such a strange feeling in the atmosphere. We did not know if there had been an accident, a hold up, an earthquake or what. We finally felt we must turn the radio and listen and see if we could find out what was going on. We did not hear anything other than what we already knew that the freeway was closed and traffic was backed up for miles. We continually prayed in the spirit, remained calm, and used the authority of the Holy Spirit to speak to the situation whatever it might have been. Suddenly the traffic started moving and they routed us across an overpass. We tried to see below if there was anything evident of why this was happening. We spoke by the inspiration of the Holy Spirit, "Situation, whatever you are, end in Jesus' Name without harm to anyone."

There were television crews everywhere with big spot lights from every station in LA County. When we checked into our motel room we turned the TV on to see what we might find out. They reported it was a hostage situation. A mental patient had hijacked a taxi and was holding the driver hostage. When he ran out of gas, the taxi stopped in one of the lanes of traffic. That is dangerous in this area of California. One part of this story is strange because the mentally ill lady was holding this hostage with the barrel of a hair dryer. We might laugh, however, if you have this round barrel in the back of your head and you are told not to turn around or I will blow your head off, just what would you do? Policemen were everywhere trying to rescue this man, but every time they would get close she would threaten to kill the driver. They were trying to keep him alive and rescue him. They had no way of knowing it was a hair dryer. You cannot imagine the confusion this caused for all those hours. No one could go anywhere within many miles of this situation. It was a drastic happening not only in the taxi, but it was also traumatic for many people who were held on the freeway without anywhere to go.

The newsman told the time when the hostage situation ended and it was at the time we passed over the overpass and spoke to the situation in the power of the Holy Spirit and spoke out of our mouth, "You are to end." We found out the freeway had been closed for eight or more hours. Deliverance had happened at the time we had entered the scene. Other people probably were praying as well; but we felt rewarded by the Lord for having obeyed the leading of the Holy Spirit to fast and pray for those days we did. Fasting gave us an authority and sensitivity to the Holy Spirit that we might not have had otherwise.

THE MOUTH

The mouth is a very powerful instrument God has given to us to create life or death. I find it interesting the main meaning of fasting is to cover the mouth. As we look at Scripture we find much said to us about this subject.

> *Matthew 12:14*
> *... out of the abundance of the heart, the mouth speaks.*

Proverbs 17:27
He that hath knowledge spareth his words.

Proverbs 10:19
He that refraineth his lips is wise.

Proverbs 15:23
A man hath joy by the answer of his mouth: and a word spoken in due season, how good is it!

Ephesians 4:29
Let no corrupt communication proceed out of your mouth, but that which is good to the use of edifying, that it may minister grace unto the hearers.

Psalm 141:3
Set a watch, O Lord, before my mouth, keep the door of my lips.

Proverbs 16:24
Pleasant words are as a honeycomb, sweet to the soul, and health to the bones.

Proverbs 15:4
A wholesome tongue is a tree of life.

When fasting, we need to appropriate the fruit of the spirit listed in *Galatians 5:22-23. But the fruit of*

What is Fasting?

the spirit is love, joy, peace, longsuffering, gentleness, goodness, faith, meekness, temperance, against such there is no law.

Since fasting and praying is a spiritual action, we must live in the spirit and walk in the spirit.

Galatians 5:26
Let us not be desirous of vain glory, provoking one another, envying one another.

Our actions speak louder than our words. If we are fasting and we are showing ugliness to those who live with us, we are **not** successfully fasting. Doing without food can make a person irritable. This is where we have to get victory over the flesh and let the Holy Spirit's fruit show instead of our flesh. The flesh yells loud when it does not get its way. The Spirit will bring great peace when He gets His way.

I have fasted supernaturally. I have done without food for as high as ten days and kept my schedule up with preaching, teaching, singing, and taking care of my everyday life. No one was suspicious of the fast. God would work it out for me in wonderful ways. Fasting according to God's plan does bring great rewards from the Lord. The **spiritual rewards** were shown in the meetings in the coming months and years.

Notes:

Chapter 2
History of Fasting

Fasting is as old as the Bible. From 1861 to 1954, a period of nearly 100 years, not a single book was published on fasting. The King of Britain called for a day of solemn prayer and fasting because of a threatened invasion by France in 1756. In February, John Wesley recorded in his journal, "The fast day was a glorious day, such as London has scarce seen since the Restoration. Every church in the city was more than half full with very solemn faced people. Surely God heareth prayer, and there will yet be a lengthening of our tranquility." In a footnote he wrote, "Humility was turned into national rejoicing for the threatened invasion by the French was averted." Quoted from John Wesley, *The Journal of the Reverend John Wesley* (London, Epworth Press 1938) p. 147

Another exerpt tells us of John Wesley not ordaining a man to the Methodist ministry unless he would commit himself to fast every Wednesday and Friday until 4:00 P.M. Reliable church tradition tells us that for seven centuries the early Church practiced fasting regularly on Wednesday and Friday of each week.

Webster defines fasting as not only prayer, but also amplified prayer. Prayer; entreaty; A formula of worship. That part of a petition, which specifies the request or desire.

The Talmud is the collection of ancient Rabbinic writings composed of the Mishnah and the Gemara, forming the basis of religious authority for Judaism.

The Mishnah is the first section of the Talmud, a compilation of early oral interpretations of the Scriptures dating from about A.D. 700. A teaching of a rabbi or other noted authority on Jewish laws. The Gemara is the second part of the Talmud consisting chiefly of commentary on Mishnah.

Prayer Watches

When speaking of prayer watches, let us refer to *Mark 13:37* which says, *And what I say unto you I say unto all, Watch.* Watch in this Scripture means to be sleepless. God does not want the Church to be sleeping. He has dealt with numerous Ministries to begin earnest heartfelt prayer for the awakening for the nations to God. The Church must be the first to awaken so that we can carry the anointing in praying for the awakening.

History of Fasting

In history, many prayer watches have taken place. Some had fasting, some had prayer and some had both prayer and fasting. It was always intense, concentrated specified time or purpose. The Moravians held one watch lasting for one hundred years in ancient Saxony (Germany). During this greatest of prayer watches, intercession was made each hour by 24 men and 24 women. Douglas Thorson describes a prayer watch that took place in the 1600's by "praying Indians". Approximately 3,000 Christians living in fourteen villages were trained by John Eliot who taught them to solemnly set apart whole days, either in giving thanks or fasting and praying with great fervor of mind and a very laborious piety.

Charles Spurgeon writes "Our seasons of fasting and prayer at the tabernacle have been high days indeed; never has Heaven's gates been wider, never have our hearts been nearer the central glory."

> *Matthew 9:15*
> *And Jesus replied to them, can the wedding guests mourn while the bridegroom is still with them? The days will come when the bridegroom is taken away from them, and then they will fast.*

We are living this time now and have been ever since Jesus departed the earth and took His place at the right hand of the Father.

Does Fasting Have Therapeutic Value?

The heathen have had a far greater knowledge of the spiritual and therapeutic value of fasting than the western peoples. If every convert from heathenism to Christianity would spend a month in true prayer and fasting, our Missionaries would have a body of such workers as they have wished for in vain, up to this point. If fasting was practiced in the churches today to the extent that it is practiced in the Orient and among the health conscious, there is every indication the Church of Jesus Christ would be blessed with major signs, healings, and miracles, all of the time instead of just a sprinkling here and there. While we have the full truth of the Gospel, we neglect the means of producing the fervency and zeal that many heathen have.

Let us remember the Scriptures in *Isaiah 58:8 AMP* which says our health shall be restored in fasting. *"Then shall your light break forth like the morning, and your healing (your restoration and the power of a new life) shall spring forth speedily; your righteousness (your rightness, your justice, and your right relationship with God) shall go before you [conducting you to peace and prosperity], and the glory of the Lord shall be your rear guard."*

We are very much in need of everything that can be

brought about by fasting. Let us not be satisfied with less than the fasting, "reward that our Father will give us openly."

Martin Luther stated, *"It was not Christ's intention to reject or despise fasting. It was his intention to restore proper fasting."*

John Wesley declares, *"First let fasting be done unto the Lord with our eye singly fixed on Him. Let our intention herein be this, and this alone, to glorify our Father which is in heaven. This is the only way we will be saved from loving the blessing more than the blessed."*

Thomas Artwright, in 1580, says, *"The holy exercise of a true fast the Sermon on the Mount on giving and praying, Jesus spoke of fasting. Giving, praying and fasting are all part of Christian Devotion. We have not more reason to exclude fasting then we do giving praying and forgiving."*

Many strategies of the enemy have been revealed in the history of nations that was stopping the progress of the Gospel. I read of one such thing in the Philippines where Christians were going to meet together to pray and 100 Pastors and Christian workers were going to come together to the prayer conference from Russia. The Philippine government would not grant the visas for them to come. While in prayer it was revealed they needed to pray, because Russia had given the Philippines much grief and the government was not seeing them as believers, but as Russians or as then known as the Soviet Union. When God revealed the strategy on how to pray, the government released them to come to the conference and gave them the proper visas. The believers stood in the gap and asked forgiveness of bitterness they had in their own hearts toward the Soviet Union.

When it says in *2 Chronicles 7:14, If my people will humble themselves and pray I will forgive their sin and heal their land.* This means exactly what is says if My people. Not the world, but God's people. The end result of this prayer strategy was 60 films of JESUS and 60 projectors were taken back to the Soviet Union to spread the Gospel.

In the 1950's there was a team of Ministers who would lead fasting and prayer conferences. This was during the Voice of Healing Revival. I saw photos of thousands of people who attended and were fasting and praying for healings to be restored to people. Is it not ironic that during the 50's it is called the Healing Revival?

Matthew 6:16-18
Moreover when ye fast, be not, as the hypocrites, of a sad countenance: for they disfigure their faces,

that they may appear unto men to fast. Verily I say unto you, they have their reward. But thou, when thou fastest, anoint thine head, and wash thy face; That thou appear not unto men to fast, but unto thy Father, which is in secret: and thy Father, which seeth in secret, shall reward thee openly.

Notes:

Notes:

Chapter 3
Is Fasting for Today?

Jesus addressed this issue with saying **when** you fast! Not **if** you fast!

We go back to this Scripture in *Matthew 6:16-18 AMP. And whenever you are fasting, do not look gloomy and sour and dreary like the hypocrites, for they put on a dismal countenance, that their fasting may be apparent to and seen by men, Truly I say to you, they have their reward in full already. But when you fast, perfume your head and wash your face. So that your fasting may not be noticed by men but by your Father, who sees in secret: will reward you in the open."*

Jesus seems to make an assumption people will fast and is giving instruction on how to do it properly. Jesus does not say, "If you fast", neither does he say, "You must fast". His Word is very simply, **"WHEN YOU FAST."**

John the Baptist's disciples asked why they fasted and the Pharisees fasted, but Jesus' disciples did not. Jesus replied in *Matthew 9:15, Can the wedding guests mourn as long as the bridegroom is with them? The days will come, when the bridegroom is taken away from them and then they will fast.*

The Kingdom of God had come among them in present power in the form of Jesus. The Bridegroom was in their midst and it was a time for feasting, not fasting. There would be a time for His disciples to fast, but not in the legalism of the old order. So when we obey the Words of the Master, fasting is definitely for today.

Notes:

Chapter 4

Purpose of Fasting

If there is any one single thing I want to point out in this chapter, it is **the motive of the heart** during a fast. Our motive must be pure. If we are fasting so that men can congratulate us, we have missed the whole point. If we are fasting so we can manipulate God's hand in prayer we have missed it also. God is the same yesterday, today and forever. When we fast and pray, we must realize we are the one who will change. We will be more sensitive to the Father's Voice. If we heed and obey we will see great victory. The **purpose** of this book is that we might have the knowledge on how to have a fast which is acceptable and chosen by God.

We just completed a declared fasting and prayer by the direction of the Holy Spirit for our nation. I knew nothing of others receiving this direction from the Holy Spirit when God started dealing with my heart to do this. I obeyed and wrote it to those who subscribe to my monthly newsletter. By the time the newsletter reached the people many others had declared the same thing. It was amazing to hear how many Ministries were calling for the people to join them in fasting and prayer during this same period of time. I got testimonies of various things that had been loosed in behalf of numerous people. In the area of finances many were released and gave their testimony. Did we have our purpose of loosening finances? That was not what we had in mind, but the mind of the Spirit of God was to help numerous people because of their obedience to fast. I had doors open for my life which I would never have tried to open. I felt such sensitivity to the Holy Spirit during this time that there were many things I was used to doing, but during this time I could not do them. I felt a lack of interest in them during this whole 40 day period. This continued on after that time in other ways. It is the purpose of shutting things out that could drown the Voice of the Lord and listening more intently to His Voice. I longed to hear His Voice more than anything else. I believe others had the same experience.

Hebrews 11:6
But without faith it is impossible to please him: for he that cometh to God must believe that He is, and that He is a rewarder of them that diligently seek him.

When we approach God, we must approach in faith and believe that He is the rewarder of them who diligently seek Him. Even if the reward is not what you expect it to be, there will be great reward to fasting and praying in faith.

Purpose of Fasting

There are numerous purposes for fasting in the Word.

In *Ezra 8:21* the purpose was for guidance, protection of children and property. *Then I proclaimed a fast there, at the river of Ahave, that we might afflict ourselves before our God, to seek of him a right way for us, and for our little ones and for all our substance.*

> *Ezra 8:23*
> *So we fasted and besought our God for this, and He heard our entreaty.*

The result was as they entreated God for these areas, He answered their prayer. As exiled Jews prepared to return to Jerusalem, Ezra called for a fast nationwide. The first purpose was to lead them in the right way by fasting for God's guidance. I believe there are times when we are in need of specific guidance that we are to fast and pray. The second purpose was for God to protect their little ones. The third purpose was for God to guard their possessions. Vast hoards of wealth and silver were saved through fasting and prayer. These great treasures that belonged to the Lord and His anointed were rescued by the power of fasting to the Lord.

Esther 4:16 shows the purpose of this fast to spare a nation of people from the plots of an evil man, Haman. The result of this fast was a whole nation was spared from a mass murderer. Esther had to have wisdom and she came to the place to say, *... and if I perish, I perish.* She had to outsmart his plan. Haman was hanged on the gallows that were made for Mordecai, Esther's Uncle. The King gave Esther Haman's house as recorded in *Esther 8:7.* What successful fasting and prayer! Still today the book of Esther is read among the Jews to remind them of the miracle of deliverance that is celebrated every year one month before the Passover.

In *Nehemiah 9* it tells about the walls of Jerusalem being broken down and the gates set on fire. Nehemiah was a selfless man with interest in God's people. God had given him favor with the King. As the King's cupbearer, he selected and tasted the King's wine to make sure it was not poisoned. When Nehemiah heard the walls of Jerusalem were broken down, he wept and mourned for many days. He was **fasting and praying** before the God of Heaven. The result of the fast was favor with the King who provided him with the finances and authority needed to rebuild the walls of Jerusalem.

As recorded in *Jonah 3:5* the people of Nineveh believed in God and proclaimed a fast and put on sackcloth from the greatest even to the least of them. The purpose of this fast was to spare a nation from the resulting judgment for that city.

Purpose of Fasting

In *Judges 20* the Benjamites were judged for having allowed a terrible sin in the city of Gibeah. A Levite's concubine had been raped and murdered by the men of the city. The Lord told the other tribes of Israel to go in battle against them. This was hard for the other tribes because this was their own people. In *Judges 20:18* it says they sought God about who would go first out against them and God said, *send Judah first.* They sent the tribe of praise out front and won the battle.

Joy had left the house of the Lord and in *Joel 1:14* they sanctified a fast and cried to the Lord. A great drought has seized the land. When the joy had gone from the house of the Lord, it affected everything. In *verse 14*, it says, *Sanctify ye a fast, call a solemn assembly, gather the elders and all the inhabitants of the land into the house of the Lord your God.*

When God said call a solemn assembly and gather the elders, it meant a day when nobody does anything but seek God. In other words, they did not eat, but all took time with God. The word *curfew* is the same word used in this passage for "a solemn assembly" and everyone had to stay at home.

In *Joel 2:12* it shows they were instructed to come with fasting from the heart to God. In *Joel 2:21* it says, *The command is be glad and rejoice for the Lord has done great things!* Joy was restored. God promised they would eat in plenty and be satisfied and praise the Name of the Lord. He told them He was their God and they were His people and He would pour out His Spirit upon them. That promise even goes to you and me still today. He repeats all this to us in *Acts 2:17 and 18.* What a fabulous fast this was!

Most of these fasting and prayers have been **corporate prayers.** Most of us know that praying in groups is called **prayer meeting.** We need to learn to fast and pray corporately to experience divine unity. Just as there is individual prayer and collective prayer there is **individual fasting** and **collective fasting**.

In *Luke 2:37* we see Anna the Prophetess worshipping and fasting. She was very old, lived in the temple and spent her life worshipping night and day with fasting and prayer. Anna had the vision of Jesus coming in redemption and she got to see Him before she died.

In the book of Acts we see groups of people fasting together for the purpose of appointing the Apostles. They would lay hands on them, pray collectively for God's guidance, then send them out on mission trips.

Chapter 5

Wrong Purposes Not Honored

As we read *Isaiah 58:3-8* we can see Israel had the wrong heart so their fasting was not honored. They questioned God about their fasting.

Isaiah 58:3-8 AMP
Why have we fasted, they say, and You do not see it? Why have we afflicted ourselves, and You take no knowledge [of it]? Behold [O Israel], on the day of your fast [when you should be grieving for your sins], you find profit in your business, and [instead of stopping all work as the law implies you and your workmen should do] you extort from your hired servants a full amount of labor. [The facts are that] you fast only for strife and debate and to smite with the fist of wickedness. Fasting as you do today will not cause your voice to be heard on high. Is such a fast as yours what I have chosen, a day for a man to humble himself with sorrow in his soul? [Is true fasting merely mechanical?] Is it only to bow down his head like a bulrush and to

spread a sackcloth and ashes under him [to indicate a condition of heart that he does not have]? Will you call this a fast and an acceptable day to the Lord? [Rather] is not this the fast that I have chosen: to loose the bonds of wickedness, to undo the bands of the yoke, to let the oppressed go free, and that you break every [enslaving] yoke? Is it not to divide your bread with the hungry and bring the homeless poor into your house when you see the naked, that you cover him, and that you hide not yourself from [the needs of your own flesh and blood?] Then shall your light break forth like the morning, and your healing (your restoration and the power of a new life) shall spring forth speedily, your righteousness (your rightness, your justice, and your right relationship with God) shall go before you [conducting you to peace and prosperity], and the glory of the Lord shall be your rear guard.

In these previous verses God laid out for them exactly what was expected from them in their fasting and prayer.

> *Jeremiah 14:12*
> *Though they fast, I will not hear their cry, and though they offer burnt offering and cereal offering [without heartfelt surrender to Me, or by offering it too late], I will not accept them. But I*

will consume them by the sword, by famine, and by pestilence.

In *verse 11 of Jeremiah 14,* the Prophets were prophesying lies in the name of the Lord. God told them pray not for this people for their good. He went so far as to say when they fast I will not hear their cry. Their pride had gotten in the way. In *Proverbs 6:16* it is listed as one of the sins God hates. A proud look, not even the action, yet, is one of the things God hates. In *Proverbs 8:13* He mentions again how He hates pride and arrogance. The reverent fear and worshipful fear of the Lord [includes] the hatred of evil, pride, arrogance, the evil way and perverted and twisted speech. When we are in the worshipful fear of the Lord we discern the things He hates and we hate them too.

As mentioned previously in *Matthew 6:17-18*, Jesus says to be seen of men when you fast is a wrong purpose or motive. In *verse 18* He makes it clear if you fast in secret: the Father will reward you in the open.

Jezebel's Fast

Here is a heathen woman who fasted with all the wrong reasons. She fasted to be able **to do evil** to a godly man with resulting judgment of being eaten by the dogs in the street. Naboath was a righteous man and she was coveting his property and set out to get it. She got her evil husband Ahab the King to help her. Because he fasted with humbleness and repented before God, he was forgiven and his life spared. It cost Jezebel her life. Both she and Ahab served idols, yet God still saw the fasts and judged them. She fasted to do evil and Ahab fasted with humility.

A year or so ago I was watching a TV news program and they showed a Muslim Cleric who was fasting and praying for the **destruction** of the United States. This is a horrible thing to do. We must keep ourselves guarded with the Blood of Jesus. Another incident I read about in the paper was where a Muslim Cleric was calling for his people to pray for a very **destructive earthquake** to come on the United States. Will God answer a prayer like that? Of course not, but destructions comes from Satan, so we must do battle in the Spirit and break these demonic assignments from Hell against our country. God will **judge a fast** just like he did Jezebel's. Actually the country this man was from had a horrible earthquake shortly thereafter. When people speak these kind of curses, they open themselves up to the powers of darkness in which they pray and they could experience the same destruction they are asking to come on someone else. We must pray for the people who are so deceived. When these things come upon innocent people, we must be praying for them. We will see miracles in this area I believe; therefore we must pray earnestly in the Holy Spirit. In the last days there will be earthquakes in diver's places. This is what the Bible speaks of, but it won't be because some deceived or twisted people prayed it upon the country.

The Priest and People Received Correction

The Priests and the people were receiving correction from God concerning their fasts. They had been fasting regularly for seventy years. They had fasted the 5th and 7th months of every year. God let them do this for seventy years when they were in exile and then asked the question, *"Did you really fast for me?"* They sent representatives to God to ask Him, *"Now that we are not in exile, should we continue to fast the fifth month separating ourselves as we have done these seventy years?"* God turned around and asked them, "Did you fast for me? When you ate and when you drank, did you eat for yourselves and drink for yourselves?" We find this happening in *Zechariah 7:1-7*. Again God points out to the people the way they treated the widow, the fatherless, and the poor. He also spoke to them about how they thought in their hearts concerning their brother. This is another example in Scripture about how religious bondage dictated their purpose and just how effective their fast was. God hates religious games. They were fasting and pretending to be holy, but they were not obeying God. Zechariah reminded them the real matter behind fasting is motive and attitude.

In *Luke 18:11-14,* Jesus tells a parable of a Pharisee who stood and prayed, *God I thank thee, I am not as other men are extortioners, unjust, adulterers or even as this publican. I fast twice a week; I give tithes of all I possess. And the publican, standing afar off, would not lift so much as his eyes to heaven, but smote upon his breast, saying, God be merciful to me a sinner.* Jesus said in no uncertain terms that the Publican was more justified. For everyone who exalts himself shall be abased. He that humbleth himself shall be exalted.

Hidden Sin is a Hindrance

In *2 Samuel 12* a story of King David's hidden sin became a hindrance.

David fasted and was not able to make any progress with God because he had hidden sin in his life. He had passed **judgment** upon himself by having Uriah killed in battle, then trying to cover his sin. He had an affair with Uriah's wife, while Uriah was dedicated to battle for the Israelites. He sinned and then sinned again to cover his actions. The story is sad because David paid a dear price for his actions. The affair resulted in a child being born. David was corrected by the Prophet Nathan who told him what would happen. Nathan told David the child would die. David was repentant and God forgave him but the ramifications kept coming. He was remorseful when the child was born, besought God, and fasted for seven days. When the child died on the seventh day, David rose up washed and anointed himself and changed his apparel and came to the house of the Lord and worshipped. His servants wondered why David fasted and wept for the child while it was alive, but when the child died he rose and ate bread. He was trying to get God's graciousness in the matter, but it did not work. The prayer was not answered in his fast because of the **judgment** of his sin. **Fasting and praying did not lift the judgment.** Nathan said to David, "You have given great occasion to the enemies of the Lord to blaspheme." David judged his own mind, will and emotions with his fasting. He brought his soul under what God wanted for him rather than what his mind was telling him which was against what God had for him. In our fasting and prayer we need to set aside time with the Lord to correct our own walk with God. If David had not covered his sin when dealt with by Nathan, we might have a different outcome.

Notes:

Chapter 6

What Does God Accept?

Luke 14:11
For whosoever exalteth himself, shall be abased; and he that humbleth himself shall be exalted.

James 4:6
He giveth more grace, wherefore he saith, God resisteth the proud, but giveth grace unto the humble.

Psalm 35:13
But as for me, when they were sick, my clothing was sackcloth. I humbled my soul with fasting and my prayer returned in my own bosom.

From these three Scriptures we see **God honors a humble heart.** Sometimes our human thinking about humility is one thing, when God's is another. In *Psalm 35:13* this word humbled means he took heed, paid attention to, spoke, sang, shouted and testified. David was speaking about false witnesses who had risen up against him. He had to bring his soul under submission to what God wanted him to do about it instead of what his flesh wanted to do. Instead of cursing or rejoicing concerning his enemies when they were sick he blessed them instead.

When Jesus was sending His disciples out He told them to bless the house where they stayed and if the house was not deserving of their blessing the blessing would return unto them. In *Luke 10:5 and 6*, this kind of blessing can take a lot of stress off our shoulders when we obey the Word of God. We do not have to be so concerned if they are deserving of the blessing or not. God will see the blessing gets back to you if you obey what He directs in blessing them.

We are made up of three parts which are **spirit, soul and body.** Our soul is where our mind, will and emotions are. Our spirit is the center of who we are in Christ and this is where we hear from God. Just like the Father, Son and Holy Spirit are three in one, He has made us three in one, one person with three parts. The following Scripture in *1 Thessalonians 5:23* tells us God wants us whole in all three areas. *And may the God of peace sanctify you wholly, and I pray God your whole spirit, and soul and body be preserved blameless unto the coming of our Lord Jesus Christ.*

Separation unto God Accepted

Nehemiah 9:1-3
Now in the twenty fourth day of this month the children of Israel were assembled with fasting and with sackcloth and earth upon them. And the seed of Israel separated themselves from all strangers, and stood and confessed their sins and the iniquities of their fathers. And they stood up in their place, and read the book of the Law of the Lord their God, and another fourth part they confessed and worshipped the Lord their God.

It was during these readings they remembered how God had led them. They recognized His power and deliverance for them. Ezra read these Scriptures and reviewed the greatness of God and He had brought them up out of Egypt. He read the past blessings of God in hard times. (See: *Nehemiah 9:6-38*)

In *verse thirteen* of this chapter he told how God had spoken from Heaven when He came down on Mt. Sinai. He gave them right judgments and true laws, good statutes, and commandments. This is a great example for us in remembering how God has brought us through tough times. This keeps us in a state of humility with the Lord. We build up our own souls when we remember how good God is.

Believing God

So the people of Nineveh believed God, and proclaimed a fast, and put on sackcloth, from the greatest of them even to the least of them. It is impossible to get results in fasting and prayer without believing God. It is not by our works we are blessed, but by faith in what God says He will do.

> *Hebrews 11:6*
> *For without faith it is impossible to please him, for he that cometh to God must believe that He is, and that He is a rewarder of them who diligently seek Him.*

We must approach fasting and prayer in faith.

Notes:

Chapter 7
How Long Should I Fast?

Being led by the Spirit is the New Testament way of fasting and prayer and **the Holy Spirit will lead you** in just how long He desires for you. There are various lengths of time for fasting as we see in Scripture, usually from one day to forty days. The following Scriptures will show the various lengths of time. In this verse they fasted one day.

> *Judges 10:26*
> *Then all the children of Israel and all the people, went up, and came unto the house of God and wept and sat there before the Lord, and fasted that day until even and offered burnt offerings and peace offerings before the Lord.*
>
> *1 Chronicles 10:12-13*
> *They arose all the valiant men and took away the body of Saul and the bodies of his sons, and brought them to Jabesh, and buried their bones under the oak in Jabesh and fasted seven days. For Saul died for his transgression which he committed against*

the Lord, even against the word of the Lord, which he kept not, and for also asking counsel of one that had a familiar spirit, to inquire of it.

Daniel 10:2-3
In those days, I Daniel was mourning three full weeks. I ate no pleasant bread, neither came flesh nor wine in me. Neither did I anoint myself at all till three whole weeks were fulfilled.

And Jesus fasted in the wilderness before He was tempted of Satan. *And when he had fasted forty days and forty nights, He was afterward an hungred. (Matthew 4:2)*

Notice in this verse that Jesus became hungry after He was released from the fast. I have had this experience when I was fasting for lengths of time. After the third day if you go further with the fast you are not hungry. You could watch anyone eat anywhere and cook food yourself and it does not bother you. The body seems to catch up with the spirit and allows this to supernaturally happen.

2 Corinthians 11:27
In weariness, and painfulness, in watching often, in hunger, and thirst, in fastings often, in cold and nakedness . . .

How Long Should I Fast?

Acts 10:30
And Cornelius said, four days ago I was fasting until this hour, and at the ninth hour I prayed in my house, and behold a man stood before me in bright clothing.

In *1 Corinthians 7:5* we see husband and wife should consent with each other before fasting over a length of time. *Defraud ye not one another, except it be with consent for a time, that ye may give yourselves to fasting and prayer, and come together again, that Satan tempt you not for your incontinency.*

In *1 Kings 19:6-8* we see Elijah fasted for **forty days.** He went in the strength of the 'angel food' for that long. The Lord was so concerned with His Prophet He made a miraculous oil cruse and a meal bin to supply Him with food. He also sent birds from Heaven to give him meat and angels prepared tables of food for this Prophet. Although many have not learned Elijah's secret and his lesson, he taught the Word to us about give no thought for tomorrow. Elijah was a miracle worker who was in contact with God. He taught us some valuable lessons if we will heed them.

How do I Determine the Length of a Fast?

Obedience is the best answer I can give you on this

one. You must be sensitive to the Holy Spirit to hear from God in any situation, whether it be in church, at home, on the job, or in the car.

Recently I was in a service and the impression of the Holy Spirit came upon me that for a certain time frame to do without a certain item. I had great joy in doing this and at the end of the time frame I did not feel released so I continued a longer time. During this fast, much was happening around me and on the inside of my heart. As I was obedient to the Holy Spirit, I was able to stay focused on God's greatness, rather than thinking on the things which were very distracting.

Daniel fasted and did not eat meat, or dessert. Some people call that a partial fast but nevertheless it was recognized by God as a fast. So whether you call it a partial fast it is still a fast that brought results.

Notes:

Chapter 8
Jesus Said Much About Fasting and Prayer

*A**nd Jesus said unto them, Can the children of the bridechamber mourn as long as the bridegroom is with them? But the days will come when the bridegroom shall be taken from them, and then shall they fast. (Matthew 9:15)* As long as they had Jesus the bridegroom with them they could not fast.

In *Matthew 6:16-18* He instructed them to be not as the hypocrites of a sad countenance who appear unto men to fast. But He told them to anoint their head and wash their face, and appear not to men to fast. Your fast should be to the Father which is in secret, and the Father shall reward you openly. This is good advice for us as well.

Jesus instructed His disciples in *Matthew 17* to use prayer and fasting when they could not cure a little boy of epilepsy.

Matthew 17:16-21
And I brought him to thy disciples, and they were

not able to cure him. And Jesus rebuked the demon and it came out of him, and the boy was cured instantly. Then the disciples came to Jesus and asked privately, Why could we not drive it out? But this kind does not go out except by prayer and fasting.

What kind was Jesus talking about? I believe He was speaking concerning their unbelief. Anytime we are facing a situation in our lives and we are having trouble believing God in that area of our lives, we need to fast and pray for a season to have our unbelief changed. The devil will test you even then.

When Jesus fasted for 40 days and nights, the devil came to tempt Him.

He fought Satan with the written Word. That is what we will have to say, **"Devil, it is written."** In this time of temptation, the devil quoted the Word but did not rightly divide it. Jesus discerned his motive and did not take his bait. Jesus did not give in to temptation and became victorious by knowing how to use the Word. So it is important for us to know which Scriptures to use when we are in battle with the forces of darkness.

In *2 Timothy 2:15* it says, *Study to show thyself approved unto God, a workman that needeth not to be ashamed, rightly dividing the word of truth.* The Amplified says it very clearly. *Study and be eager and do your utmost to present yourself to God approved (tested by trial), a workman who has no cause to be ashamed, correctly analyzed and accurately dividing [rightly handling and skillfully teaching] the word of Truth.*

So if we can skillfully handle the Word of God, then we may be able to do it incorrectly as well. As we read the Word, pay attention to who is talking, to whom they are speaking, and what they are talking about. This will help you understand the Word of God and present it accurately to others.

I pray that the Holy Spirit will give you clear understanding of what the Word of God says about prayer and fasting so that you will become skillful in handling the Word of Truth.

Notes:

Notes:

Chapter 9

Corporate Oneness

Corporate in the Webster's Dictionary means combined or united into one body, collective.

We find at the church at Antioch they were ministering to the Lord in worship and fasting and the Holy Spirit spoke. There is much power in the unity of ministering to the Lord together.

In *Acts 13:2-3 As they ministered to the Lord and fasted, the Holy Ghost said, Separate me Barnabas and Saul for the work whereunto I have called them. And when they had fasted and prayed, and laid their hands on them, they sent them away.*

Opposition would come against the Word of God as they preached it. Paul was so filled with the power of God he spoke to Elymas who was against them and said, *"behold the hand of the Lord is upon you and you will be blind for a season."* Great boldness was upon Paul as a manifestation of the presence of God upon him. (See: *Acts 13:9-11*)

In the early days of the Church, Paul and the disciples prayed over the men in the churches. *And when they had appointed and ordained elders for them in each church with prayer and fasting, they committed them to the Lord in Whom they had come to believe [being full of joyful trust that He is the Christ, the Messiah].* (Acts 14:23 AMP)

We see here empowerment for the Gospel to go to the nations through fasting and prayer that many should come to know the Messiah.

Fasting saved the city of Nineveh after Jonah cried that it would be overthrown. After he repented and returned from Joppa, Jonah went to Nineveh and preached to the people and they believed God. The King of that land proclaimed the whole city to fast and pray from the greatest to the least. (See: *Jonah 3:5*)

What were the results of this corporate fast? The people were saved from destruction and their prayers reached God. *And God saw their works, that they turned from their evil way; and God repented of the evil, that He had said that he would do unto them, and he did it not. (Jonah 3:10)* **AMAZING!**

Their fasting and prayer changed God's mind about His judgment. This says a lot about corporate fasting and prayer. Two things happened in this corporate fast. (1) Over a million people were spared and (2) God repented of the judgment he had said would come unto them.

Could the things going wrong in our nation be changed by this kind of fast? That is why we pray for those in authority to be directed by the Spirit of God. We must continue to pray for the 'awakening' in this country and other nations. In the United States of America it is time for repentance.

This year the Holy Spirit spoke to my heart a very comforting thing: "This nation is in the hands of the prayers". I have stepped up my prayer life and so many others have as well. We are seeing dramatic changes and the awakening of the Church is definitely in high gear around the world. Let us not give up or give in. THIS IS OUR TIME!

Notes:

Chapter 10
The Rewards of Fasting

In various Scriptures we have already covered in this book, we see many **rewards** but the one Scripture that lists the most rewards is found in *Isaiah 58*. In this chapter, God speaking through the Prophet is letting them know the fast they themselves have chosen is not the kind of fast God Himself has in mind. He then explains to them what a God-chosen fast looks like. When we fast we certainly want the kind of fast God has chosen, not the kind that leads nowhere.

In *verse 6* God says the fast I have chosen loosens the bands of wickedness. *Is this not the fast I have chosen: to loose the chains of injustice and untie the cords of the yoke, to set the oppressed free and break every yoke? (Isaiah 58:6 NIV)*

Good things should happen as a result of a God-chosen fast. We loosen the bands of wickedness. There are four things the God-chosen fast is supposed to look like in this *verse 6*. We will see the (1) Loosing the bands of wickedness, (2) Undo the burdens, (3)

Letting the oppressed go free and (4) Breaking the yokes. Wow, what victory we shall see when we plug into the God-kind of fast. These rewards mentioned can be in prayers for ourselves, for those around us, or even for nations of this world. Our country needs a continual fast of the believers who hold this nation in their hands through the power of prayer.

Isaiah 10:27 speaks of the yoke being destroyed because of the anointing. In the New Testament it speaks of the anointing abiding within us.

I John 2:27 in the Amplified Bible states the anointing permanently dwells in you. What a promise we have about this anointing. I believe there are things we can do to increase the anointing on our life. When we fellowship with the Lord, the anointing is increased in order to deal with things that break the bonds of wickedness. God entrusts us with this anointing, but it carries a responsibility. This Scripture also speaks of our having an unction from the Holy One. The word *unction* and the word *anointing* are the same Greek word, **Chrisma**. [This words means anything smeared on; a scented ointment of thicker consistency than sweet oil or perfume. *(Dake King James Notes)*]

We should be an odor pleasing to God. We have all heard the saying, she or he sure 'spreads it on'. In that

The Rewards of Fasting

sense, it means they are really stretching things or flattering you. It usually is some kind of manipulation tactic to win influence with someone. However, we should be a sweet-smelling odor anointed to spread love to the nations. Load up on the goodness of God and 'Spread it on' to everyone around us!

The next **reward** of fasting chosen by God **is our health** shall spring forth speedily. We will address health issues and fasting in the next chapter, but I wanted to let you know this is one of the rewards of fasting and prayer.

Undoing of **heavy burdens** is another reward or blessing of fasting and prayer. Doing the 7 things listed in *Isaiah 58:6-7* ensures that you will have a fast that is blessed by God:

1. Loose the bands of wickedness
2. Undo the heavy burdens
3. Let the oppressed go free
4. Break every yoke
5. Deal your bread to the hungry
6. Bring the poor to your house
7. Hide not thyself from your own flesh

More rewards are listed ... *thy righteousness shall go before thee; the glory of the Lord will be your rear guard. You will cry and God will answer you. When your darkness will be as the noon day. (Isaiah 58:8)*

The righteousness of God is what we are through Jesus Christ. This will be made manifest in our daily lives. Guidance will come.

> *Isaiah 58:11-12*
> *The Lord will guide you continually. He will satisfy you in drought. He will make your bones fat. You will be like a watered garden (productive and fruitful). You will be like an unfailing spring of water. Freshness will be on our life. Draining of our resources in God will be impossible due to our God chosen fast. Our waste places will be built. The waste lands will be restored to a habitable state and the blessings that should have been enjoyed for many generations shall be ours. You will raise up the foundations of many generations. You will be called the repairer of the breach and the restorer of paths to dwell on.*

If the Jews did the things in *verse 14*, the next promise comes. *You will delight yourself in the Lord. He will cause us to ride upon the high places of the earth. I will feed you with the heritage of Jacob your father, for I have spoken it from my mouth.*

The Rewards of Fasting

These **rewards** or blessings are a guideline for us to follow as an example. Of course most of them line up with the New Testament teachings which produce good fruit in our lives. The **rewards** of fasting far outweigh any fleshly pleasure we might think we are giving up.

Notes:

Notes:

Chapter 11

Health and Fasting

Isaiah 58:8a
Then shall thy light break forth as the morning, and thy health shall spring forth speedily.

Many doctors especially those who go the route of less medication promote fasting for restoration of health. Dr. Don Colbert is a spirit filled doctor who has numerous books on subjects relating to restoration of our health and he promotes fasting as a method of healing in certain cases. In his book, *The Seven Pillars of Health,* Dr. Colbert shares some information about fasting.

"As a doctor, I witness the benefits of fasting all the time. Fasting cleanses the body from built-up chemicals, metals, and other toxins. Fasting revitalizes you in every way: mentally, physically and spiritually. It also allows the overburdened liver to "catch up" on its detoxification work. The fast I recommend most often is a fresh, juiced organic vegetable and fruit fast as opposed to a water–only fast. A juice fast creates an alkaline environment for your body's cells and tissues so they can begin to release toxins on a cellular level and eliminate them through the body's channels of elimination. I recommend fasting just one day a month to only a few days a month. However, a three-week juice fast once a year may be very beneficial. I offer specific fasting programs in my books: *Get Healthy Through Detox and Fasting, Fasting Made Easy, and Toxic Relief* (p. 177).

Dr. Colbert further stated:

"The most important foundation of a stress-less life is meditation on the Bible. I sometimes have my patients fast television, magazines, and radio for a certain period of time and memorize Scriptures, especially *1 Corinthinans 13,* the "love chapter". . . read it aloud and insert their name into it" (p. 255).

I referred in the previous chapter to a doctor who prescribes fasting to give the body a break and allow it to heal itself. Numerous believing doctors today are learning more about fasting and are developing techniques of healing that are largely overlooked by medical schools.

Some folks have had the 'religious idea' that if you were sick you were somehow glorifying God or that

Health and Fasting

He was using it as a way of chastening you. There is no Scripture for such thinking. If sickness is the will of God; then, every physician would be a lawbreaker, every trained nurse would be defying God. And every hospital and health resort would be a house of rebellion; instead of a house of mercy.

If you are having difficulty believing God for your healing, fasting is a way of placing you before the promises of God concerning your healing. In *verse 8* it speaks of our health being restored speedily. During the time of fasting, meditate upon the healing Scriptures; take them for yourself, and use them to benefit yourself in God. That process will strengthen our faith. *Faith comes by hearing and hearing by the Word of God. (Romans 10:17)*

Fasting can be a tool we use for restoration in our spirit, soul and body. We are facing emotional trials in our nation today that past generations did not know anything about. The stress level is way off the scales in comparison to the way our ancestors lived. Life's pressures are mounting up; therefore, we must learn to live by the guidelines God has given us in His Word. Some things are a result of not eating properly, complication of diseases and breaking down of the nervous system. When other methods fail, fasting along with prayer does bring healing. It takes faith to remove these mountains and cast them into the sea. We cannot doubt in our hearts. When we fast for health restoration, we should pray, fast, rest and exercise moderately.

Notes:

Chapter 12
Common Sense in Fasting

It is important to learn the physical aspects of fasting as not to hurt yourself or cause others around you undue stress. There are some good healthy guidelines I have learned and want to share with you. It is important to use wisdom in this process of fasting. Wisdom is gained through God's Word and applied to the the knowledge you have on a matter.

God ordained a combination of fasting and resting for the Day of Atonement. Leviticus records God's ordination for that day.

> *Leviticus 16:29-31 AMP*
> *And this shall be a statute for ever unto you, that in the seventh month, on the tenth day of the month, [that's the Day of Atonement] ye shall afflict your soul [by fasting] and do not work at all whether it be one of your own country or a stranger that sojourneth among you. For on that day shall the priest make an atonement for you, to cleanse you, that ye may be clean from all your*

sins before the Lord. It shall be a Sabbath of rest unto you, and ye shall afflict your souls, by a statute forever."

So fasting is giving the body a rest from performing and giving the soul a break as well. Thank God that now Jesus has cleansed us from sin and we can go into the throne room anytime, anywhere and fellowship with Him. There is preparation of heart and mind to prepare us for a fast.

Dealing with the Toxins

If you forget to take out the trash for a week, the smell of it can fill the house. Toxins have built up in your body for months and it is good for you to recognize that they will be coming from your body during the fasting period. You may experience different smells from your body as they come out through your bladder, skin, and bowel functions. When this happens sometimes your body may not feel so good. This usually passes within a few hours, if it occurs. If you know what is happening, then this information can be of comfort to you. If you have any doubt as to what is going on with your body, then check with your doctor. I am just telling you my personal experience.

Withdrawals

Some people have withdrawals from caffeine. Usually, when this happens it is common to have headaches. It might be good to withdraw from caffeine slowly. Many years ago when I was fasting for a length of time, I had the desire to drink coffee to leave me. I had been drinking an enormous amount of coffee everyday without realizing it. I made a caffeine-rich pot of coffee in the morning and drank it all during the day. I had not set my mind to stop drinking coffee, nor did I realize how much I had been drinking until I was supernaturally delivered from it. Is it wrong to drink coffee? No, I do not believe it is. I was out of balance with it and the Holy Spirit made the adjustment. It was many years before I ever drank it again. Now, when I occasionally drink coffee, I prefer to drink decaf.

Sometimes you may feel nauseated, especially if you are not used to fasting without food. If that happens, just take a bite of something light, perhaps a protein or vegetable and continue on your journey of fasting. Because of our lifestyles many of us will experience bodily symptoms that we do not understand. Some common things that are possible are headaches, dizziness, or nausea. In most cases what is happening is the blood in your body which normally takes up in the process of digestion is now liberated from that and begins to work in other areas to clear them up.

Prepare for the Fast

Some people who do a partial fast will give up these foods for a period of time: chocolate candy, soft drinks, all desserts, or anything you really enjoy. It can be not watching your favorite TV program and giving that time to the Lord in prayer. Everyone has something they can really make a heart decision about and let it go. It is an inward matter between you and God. When we overeat, we are pushing our bodies to do extra work digesting unneeded food. It isn't able to do the other things that it needs to be doing. One of the ways we can fool our stomachs is by **drinking water;** instead of, thinking we have to eat. One thing is for sure, there is no condemnation in Christ, so if these symptoms become too much, just do what you have to do and get back to fasting as soon as possible. If you are employed, you may have to temporarily stop the fast, but return as soon as you can.

I believe in **supernatural fasting** with God and His Word there to help you. The Holy Spirit has to be along side of us during the fasting and prayer time or else it is in vain. In my younger days of fasting, I would sense I should fast for three days or whatever the Lord led me to do. Sometimes, in the beginning, I would have to go to bed and after a day all the desires of food were gone. I finally got to the place where I had no difficulty at all. After three days, you will not be hungry at all. You have 'broken the barrier' that hinders and you will feel rejuvenated. Fasting can become **exciting and enjoyable**, because it is an accomplishment both spiritual and physical.

It is important to consume a lot of liquid during a fast, especially **pure water.** Your sense of taste will become keener as you begin noticing an unpleasant taste in the drinking water; therefore I suggest purified drinking water for a fast. Sometimes **honey and lemon** in water will change the taste and help in purifying the system. You may drink boullions, broths, fruit juices, and other nutritional things. It is your decision and you are not under bondage one way or the other.

Stomach acids will cause your breath to smell really bad. Keep **breath mints** close at hand so others can handle it if you have this happen. You may not smell it yourself, but others will. If you are going to be around people, you must remember to use a flavored breath mint.

Paul mentions in *2 Corinthians 6:3-4a, Giving no offense in any thing, that the ministry be not blamed; but in all things approving ourselves as the ministers of God ...* We know he followed scriptural guidelines as he wanted to have a productive fasting and prayer time.

Overeating

Do not stock up by eating more food you like before you start a fast. That is not wise, in fact **slightly lighter than normal** meals are best for the day or two **before a fast begins.** If beginning a longer fast, it is best not to drink coffee or tea three days before you start. If the last meal in the stomach is fresh fruits and vegetables, you will have less difficulty with your digestive system operating in a flowing manner. **Begin with a partial fast** of 24 hours before the real fast begins. Eat lightly, lunch to lunch, drinking fresh fruit juice. As the fast begins, you will be performing your regular duties outwardly, but inwardly you will be in prayer, adoration, singing and worshipping God.

Another practical thing to note is when you fast any length of time over a day, your bowels will not perform as normal. However, once you start eating, they will start functioning again. If you started your fast by eating fruits and vegetables before, you should not have constipation problems when the fast is ended. To go without fluids is not advisable because it can be dangerous physically and mentally. I have met a few people who have done this, but it is better to use wisdom with your body unless God directs.

One place in the Scriptures the Jews were told not to eat

or drink for three days. In *Esther 4:16* Esther told her Uncle Mordecai, *"Go gather together all the Jews that are present in Shushan, and fast ye for me, and neither eat nor drink three days, night or day. I also and my maidens will fast likewise ..."* This was a very desperate situation and it required desperate measures. Three days is the only place in the Scripture I have seen this mentioned of doing without food and water.

You will be **more sensitive** to God's Voice during a fast, so bind the forces of evil from speaking to your mind and giving you imaginations. Cleanse your mind with the Word of God. Plead the blood of Jesus over your spirit, soul and body during the fast. **Keep focused** on the things of God, rightly dividing the Word of Truth. Be sensitive to the Holy Spirit as you speak to your family and other Christians during this time of fasting. Keep your thoughts on the Lord. Remember to be aware; the enemy came to Jesus after He had fasted for 40 days and nights. Resist him steadfast with the Word. I have found when I have fasted sometimes at the end of the fast, the enemy has presented himself to me in some kind of spiritual attack. Satan came to Jesus when He had completed His fast. Satan used the Word against Jesus, but Jesus knew the Word more accurately and used it back on him. During this time you have gained spiritual strength and you may need to be prepared to use it.

I had an occasion one time where there was a crisis in Ministry and I fasted and prayed for three days about the matter. The whole time I was fasting and praying, the person who had caused the problem was trying to reach me by phone to resign from the position they were striving for. This position was too important to them in name and it was putting them in strife with others. I did not hear from them until the fast ended. I still was glad I had fasted in obedience to God. The victory was won without a fight. PTL!

Diabetics

Those who are medically told not to do without food are persons who have diabetes. Others are expectant mothers and those with heart issues. In these cases, it is best to get medical advice

Notes:

Chapter 13

How to Break a Fast

You should break a fast with fruit and vegetable juice in small amounts at first. Remember your stomach has shrunk considerably and the entire digestive system has gone into a kind of hibernation. Next, begin to eat fruit, fresh salads, and cooked vegetables. A good guideline is: for every day you have fasted, drink juices and eat lightly for that many days afterwards. Do not start to eat again by eating greasy, fat or heavy foods. Avoid all salad dressings, grease, and starch. Extreme care should be taken not to overeat. I have seen many people do the opposite of what I am telling you.

One time I was on the foreign mission field and the Lord spoke to me about fasting for 10 days and keep on preaching every night. I had **supernatural help**. When the fast had ended, a lady who did not know we were fasting and also did not realize it was our American holiday of Thanksgiving, invited us to her home for dinner. It was the first meal I had in 10 days. I did not get to do what I advised you to do about breaking the fast. There is an exception to all of this natural stuff. I had broken the fast earlier in the day but had no idea what to expect for dinner that night. She had prepared turkey, dressing, ligonberry sauce, (taste similar to our cranberry sauce) boiled potatoes, vegetables, etc. In Scandinavia the desserts are out of this world. They were delicious and beautiful. I prayed and asked the Lord to protect me in this breaking of the fast. I did not get sick or have any of the ill effect of breaking the fast this way; however, I did not overeat. This whole meal meant a great deal to me. It was the Lord blessing us especially for having obeyed Him. She did not know our Thanksgiving custom and when we told her, she was abundantly blessed as well. This is the only occasion I remember out of seven years of going there regularly, this kind of dinner was prepared for us. Lots of wonderful meals were spread before us as these people were very hospitable, but not turkey and all the traditional trimmings. It was such a blessing to us.

Anywhere between 21 days and 40 days, **hunger pains** can return. This is the first sign of starvation and the pains signal the body has used up reserves and is beginning to draw on living tissue. The **fast should be broken** at this time. Another thing you may feel in your body, is feeling cold more easily because your metabolism is not producing the usual amount of heat.

How to Break a Fast

If you have never fasted even one meal, to take on a 2 week fast, is not God's way. So, to start out on a forty day fast without ever having fasted before is not a wise way of approaching fasting. One way to be successful in your first attempt is to skip your dinner or supper. Then do not eat anything else the rest of the day until breakfast. You will have gone approximately 18 hours.

Notes:

Notes:

Chapter 14
A Fasted Life

F ood does not sustain us, God does. In fasting we are not as much abstaining from food as we are feasting on the Word of God.

> *Joshua 1:8*
> *This book of the Law shall not depart out of your mouth, but you shall meditate upon it day and night, that you may observe and do according to all that is written in it. For then you shall make your way prosperous, and then you shall deal wisely and have good success.*

We started this book out by saying it is not all together what you put in your mouth as it is what we allow to go out of our mouth. If, in our fasting, we are putting the Word of God in our mouth, we will also be speaking out of the abundance of our hearts. Since fasting means to **cover over the mouth**, it is very important what we speak and think during this time. Fasting is more than just abstaining from food. Those things that may **mean too much to us** are those things we should prayerfully abstain from. This is living a fasted life.

When Jesus did the will of His Father, it was food that His disciples knew not of. In fasting and prayer we should find that food from the Father.

> *John 4:32-34 AMP*
> *But He assured them, I have food (nourishment) to eat of which you know nothing and have no idea. So the disciples said one to another, Has someone brought him something to eat? Jesus said to them, My food (nourishment) is to do the will (pleasure) of Him Who sent Me and to accomplish and completely finish His work.*

Paul, the Apostle, put his physical body under control by prayer and fasting. As a Minister of Gospel, he wanted the people to see the reality of Jesus in his life. *But like a boxer, I buffet my body and subdue it, for fear that after proclaiming to others the Gospel and things pertaining to it, I myself should become unfit [not stand the test, be unapproved and rejected as a counterfeit].* Fasting gives you added strength to overcome the flesh.

In this teaching concerning fasting, we have covered different aspects of fasting. It should be **a lifestyle for the believer,** being obedient to the Holy Spirit as He leads us in fasting, or as we decide to fast a certain time for a certain thing. I heard a report where a doctor friend of mine fasts two meals a day, one day a week, to hold up his family of six children in special prayer.

Notes:

Notes:

Conclusion

We have studied all the wrong reasons for fasting and the right ones as well. We have covered what God will accept and what He does not accept. We have learned how whole groups and nations prayed for deliverance from certain enemies and how God answered their prayer. We have seen the value of fasting for our own personal guidance or for a nation, protection, and safety of our children.

In this teaching, we have seen fasting is for today. We have heard some interesting history about fasting from the Bible and from earlier centuries. God wants us to humble ourselves, come closer to Him, and understand His Word. We will find His will in our lives, seek healing for our bodies, or get deliverance from evil spirits. We have learned to seek God's intervention in a crisis which cannot be handled by ordinary means and to intercede and pray on the behalf of others. We have discovered that our motive is more important than the length of time spent fasting and that it is wise to build up to a longer period of fasting over time and experience.

Fasting and prayer has changed my life and moved things on Earth for me and my family. God does answer prayer. Lots of times I have seen great things happen immediately; other times I have had delayed victories. **It takes faith** to fast, **faith** to break the fast, and **faith** to believe God when you do not see a hoped-for answer.

I feel it is time for **the Church** to step up to the plate in prayer and fasting and carry us through these last days before our Lord's return. Just recently the Holy Spirit led me to call a corporate fast and prayer and I have heard so many victorious testimonies from those who participated. I have imparted to you what God has given me about prayer and fasting and pray that you are enriched on every side. ***Blessed coming in and blessed going out*** is the promise of the Lord when we obey Him. (See: *Deuteronomy 28:30*)

Living a fasted life is a **victorious life**, living above the dictates of the flesh. Our Christian life will become **stronger in faith**, our hearing more sensitive, and our thoughts more in line with the Word of God as we **'cover our mouth'** and dedicate a special time of fasting to the Lord.

About the Author

- Rachel Jeffries graduated from Rhema Bible Training Center in 1996.

- Rachel has spoken and taught in 13 nations: USA, Norway, Denmark, Finland, Sweden, Romania, Poland, Russia, Israel, Canada, Mexico, Cuba and Africa.

- She is a musician, song writer, guest and conference speaker, and author. Her book, Capture A City Through Praise, was a best seller and is published in several languages.

- As a traveling minister she pioneered many of God's works in the USA and other nations.

- She has appeared on television in the USA, Canada and Norway.

- She is ordained with A Glorious Church Fellowship, Billye Brim Ministries.

• Contact Information •

Dr. Rachel V Jeffries has a TV program called, REVIVAL WITH DR. RACHEL JEFFRIES on streaming network, KBTV at 6:30 P.M. CST or 7:30 P.M. EST

Rachel Jeffries International Ministries has a channel on YOUTUBE as **Rachel V Jeffries**. We invite you to subscribe and receive notifications. Be sure you click on *Subscribe* as well as click on *Notifications*.

You will find AMAZING LOVE CD, and current broadcasts, as well as past ones.

Rachel Jeffries International Ministries' page on Facebook and streaming every Tuesday at 6:pm (CST).

WIDOWS WITH PURPOSE page on FB where blogs are written with encouragement to widows and widowers.

Rachel Jeffries International Ministries
P.O. Box 815
Hollister, MO 65673

This ministry is open to speaking in conferences, Bible Schools as well as churches and other events. All ministry inquiries may be sent to:
rachel@rjim.org
as well as through the website,
www.rjim.org

● Other Media Available ●
by Dr. Rachel V Jeffries

Rachel is a songwriter and recording artist.

Her CDs AMAZING LOVE A 2 CD PACKAGE AND ATMOSPHERE OF PRAYER AND WORSHIP

Available on ITUNES and SPOTIFY as well as the ministry website: *www.rjim.org*

● Other Books Available ●
by Dr. Rachel V Jeffries

CAPTURE A CITY THROUGH PRAISE
A handbook on intercessory praise.

This is a teaching of the highest form of prayer in spiritual warfare and how victorious living is possible through praise.

Offered in Paperback and Kindle ebook

Amazon.com

PITIFUL OR POWERFUL
THE CHOICE IS YOURS

Is the first book in a series called,
THE ROAD TO WHOLENESS.

Offered in Paperback and Kindle ebook
Amazon.com

You can overcome in every area of life. Dr. Rachel Jeffries shows you how with simple straightforward lessons from life experiences and God's unchanging Word.

Offered in Paperback and Kindle ebook

Amazon.com

www.ingramcontent.com/pod-product-compliance
Lightning Source LLC
Chambersburg PA
CBHW070654050426
42451CB00008B/345